PRAISE FOR *Night Visions* by Marsha M. Nelson

"In *Night Visions*, Marsha M. Nelson threads the cycle of the outer world — Things die in winter — through the cycle of the spirit-self — The heart is . . . breakable — with the ability to rebound. This collection is evidence of her deep-seated spiritual roots and how her faith has given her wings to fly above difficult things and rest on branches of victory."

> —Loretta Diane Walker, Author of *Word Ghetto*
> and *In This House*

"If the heart is the meeting point between body and soul, this book of poems is a tender yet insistent record of what happens when an attentive pilgrim journeys there and experiences the heart's turbulence and beatitude. It is a place of tension and grace, a place of separation and conjoining. Reading *Night Visions*, we experience first hand that part of us which responds to the gravitational forces of material existence, and is beguiled by its lilt; and at the same time, that 'other' part of us which seeks to soar heavenward on transcendant wings. "Keep your heart open through everything," says Rumi, in the epigaph to the author's poem "There is Purpose in Pain." In poem after poem, Marsha Nelson exposes the contours of doing just that."

> —George Wallace,
> Writer in Residence, Walt Whitman Birthplace

"Marsha Nelson's poems, in her new poetry book, *Night Visions*, journey through the sacred and profane, sacraments and secular life. I am especially mesmerized by the dark language reminiscent of Robert Frost's in her poem "Rebirth," where "Winter came fierce this year, / its frigid fingers gripping." And who cannot identify with the sadness expressed in "I Thought it was Love," in which "When lighter days morph / into meaningless nights, / it's like sunshine turning into rain"? Not coincidentally, this is the poem that won her the first place award in the Nassau County Poet Laureate's 2016 contest. Marsha has a unique poetic voice and presence that has matured greatly since she was my student in the early part of the twenty-first century, during which time she published her chapbook, *All Rise*."

—Lynn Cohen, Associate Professor of English, Suffolk County Community College, Author of *Dreams and Dreamers*

"In *Night Visions*, Marsha M. Nelson uses her spiritual voice to assess the material world around her: "Moon trails me by night,/clarity and truth by day." She is acutely aware of how the physical and spiritual worlds collide and affect us kinetically: "Kin to the universe, /ancient as time./ Power connects us." Her Israel poems both intrigued and transported me back to where I: "Walk the rugged stone path..."/ "In front of the Western Wall." Each of these special poems is an ode to the remarkable land that is Israel. Her poem "Yad Vashem" is a tribute to the memory of all fallen Holocaust victims: "Lambs in the embracing arms of Janusz Korczak, /now serving his ghetto orphans in the afterlife." *Night Visions* is a must read."

—Lana Bakhash
Co-founder of the Babylonian Jewish Center in Great Neck

NIGHT VISIONS

Poems by
Marsha M. Nelson

BLUE LIGHT PRESS ◆ 1ST WORLD PUBLISHING

1st WORLD
PUBLISHING

SAN FRANCISCO ◆ FAIRFIELD ◆ DELHI

WINNER OF THE **2016** NASSAU COUNTY
POET LAUREATE SOCIETY AWARD

NIGHT VISIONS
Copyright ©2017 by Marsha M. Nelson

1ST WORLD LIBRARY
PO Box 2211
Fairfield, Iowa 52556
www.1stworldpublishing.com

BLUE LIGHT PRESS
www.bluelightpress.com
Email: bluelightpress@aol.com

BOOK, COVER DESIGN
Melanie Gendron

AUTHOR PHOTO
Curtis Charles Photography

FIRST EDITION

ISBN: 978-1-4218-3788-8

In memory of my Father, Winston Nelson,
and my Grandfather, William Gittens.

Thank you both
for shaping my early childhood love for animals.
Because of this, my work with animals is one of my life's
greatest passions, along with poetry and drama.

Special Thanks

I am so grateful to my mentor, Diane Frank, for believing in me and my potential to uncover the "poem within the poem" and for teaching me to paint pictures with words. She has been the midwife of my gift with poetry. The first time I met Diane at one of her readings, she autographed my book: "You have the soul of a poet." This has been the catalyst for me to keep writing poetry. Thank you to Lynn Cohen, my professor from Hofstra University, who taught me all the basics and fine-tuning skills of poetry. Thank you for introducing me to Diane Frank and to the world of the Performance Poetry Association, with Cliff Bleidner as the founder.

Thank you to Lorraine Conlin for welcoming me back into the Association after I had taken a long break.

Thank you to my family and friends, who support me in so many ways. I thank God for you.

ACKNOWLEDGEMENTS

Grateful acknowledgement is made to the editors of the following anthologies in which some of these poems were previously published:

Literary Review of the Performance Poets Association, NCPLS Review, The Long Island Quarterly, Poets Almanac 2017 and *Bards Annual 2016, 2017.*

"Hold fast to dreams, for if dreams die, life is a
Broken-winged bird that cannot fly."

—Langston Hughes

CONTENTS

Baptism

Sun, Moon and Stars,
the ancients, whisper softly
in the ears of
my spirit.

The warmth of their ethereal
light vibrates alive in me,
caressing my face, lighting
my path.

I long for yet cannot find
the miracle that happens
when words move me.

A piece of the heavens,
manna for my soul.
It's poetry to feel the cool
smooth stone between my fingers,
and watch as it skips
the surface of still waters.
One ripple affects us all,
but it's quiet here, standing
on the Rock.

I sense years of formation,
witness rebirth
as souls go down,
emerge changed.

The ancients testify
looking over the sea of people.
There is life in these waters.

Rebirth

Winter came fierce this year,
its frigid fingers gripping.

I'm always in awe of its cool
white beauty, milky and pure,
yet recoil from its harsh reality,
lonely and cold.

Things die in winter.

Watching from my window,
the sun sends warm buttery kisses
over my face and chest.
Soft powder falls
quietly from a weighed-down branch,
lush and green
with life last season,
now dry and frozen.

Crystal shimmers blow past
my window.
Buried deep beneath
is the bud of new birth.

I think of you, muscular and strong,
moving props and acting, laughing.
Busy behind the prison walls,
helping blind eyes to see
and soothing the fears
at Christmas about children left behind.

That was last spring,
but as the leaves withered
and fell, and the chill
tinged the air,
I did not sense your unease
or know of your disease.

I watched as your weight shed.
Your frame withered and my heart
turned to dread.
I prayed for the breath
of life to blow on you.

It's almost spring again,
and the promise of life captures me.
I stand in awe
watching nature's symphony
played out
in the same hospital you died in.
I watch as my cousin holds
his firstborn son in his arms
and I marvel at Rebirth.

Power

Kin to the universe
ancient as time,
power connects us.

Raging, at other times mild,
yin and yang.
Energy that moves the clouds
over the vast expanse of the sky.
Cracks through ashen and pearly nebulas,
slivers of luminous columns,
radiating a path towards
the tumultuous seas.

Transcending the usual,
kindling a darker side of you and me.
A bolt of lightning,
pieces of the heavens.
Fallen in a haze of feathered confusion.
Seething in black fury,
a lost estate imprisoned.

A slow mist rising,
thick emerald turf and underbrush,
tall luscious apple trees,
flowers the colors of a rainbow.
Earth newly born, when all was
innocent and young.

Then deceit slithered in.
Venomous hate smoldering in its sinews,
bent on retribution.
God's creation groaned
from the spilt blood of Abel.

Birth pangs of a universe,
a polluted bloodline.
Mixed breed of the divine,
Immortal and humanity,
shaking God's natural order to calamity.

Two warriors suspended between
two dimensions.
David and Goliath.
One knighted by light,
the other by darkness.
Power within the battle cry,
Mastery against a champion.
A soon-to-be King wins the throne
with one shot of his smooth stone.

Two witnesses of Revelation
anointed with mystery weapons;
both citizens of a heavenly kingdom
with the power to breathe fire
on their opponents.
Victory over a bitter seed
protecting God's descendants.

Gravity

The essence of past, present and future,
hangs on a metaphysical thread
that expands infinitely.

Like the roar of the ocean to the shore,
we attract each other magnetically.
We are the heart of this universe,
web of souls,
parts of the body of Christ.
He is the cord that knits us together.
If the spine is severed,
how can we stand as one?

There is a force waging war for our souls.
It surrounds us intentionally,
seeking to penetrate our veils
that hide the gift within.

The wind thunders through
the top branches of my neighbor's tree,
like a freight train.
It sweeps a tidal wave in my soul,
storms of confusion.
I'm shaken,
but I know how to ride the breakers.
At other times, an insidious spirit
lurks behind a smirk or a whisper,
tentacles far reaching.

I'm flying again, free floating as
I slip the noose from my neck,
the flames of hell still licking
at my heels.
I go from glory to glory.

There is a fire within my belly
some form of gravity,
I can only describe as your
Holy Spirit.

War of the Heart

*"All things have a hollow center
so secret and sacred it can't be entered,
the heart of an open rose."*
—Nynke Passi

The heart is an unstoppable power,
always hopeful.
Sometimes breakable,
but with the unique ability to rebound.
Heedless, it wants what it wants.

It's the core of my being —
fragile, resilient and headstrong.
Flesh and blood versus spirit,
craving ambitious adventures
seeking deep unconditional love,
Yet bringing me to my knees.
Wayward, a serpent's claw
leaving me in tattered shreds.

Beguiling sylph,
I'm enchanted by your lilt.
One splash of a crystal droplet,
swells the cerulean current.
a gentle heat casting its spell
and the seduction is complete.

Who will bring me back?
Stretched too thin in unknown dimensions,
on a silver cord
soul flight
on a strange bird's wing.

Walls

We build them like skyscrapers,
high and skillful,
standing erect and aloof.
Soldiers digging trenches,
laying siege to our fears and misgivings.
A conundrum of victory versus self-defeat.

Sometimes, I put up barriers,
measuring the sting of heartache
at arm's length.
Unaware that I may have blocked
what could have been
the best thing in my life.

My heart swaddles wounds as if
protecting a newborn babe,
but it has formed scars.
Each blemish teaches me
great lessons of life and love,
bitter and sweet.
So I learn to unfold my arms,
open them wide and embrace
who life has to offer,
their entrances and exits.

I want to taste life with all my senses,
lifelines which connect,
heart to heart.
We have the ability
to shut each other down,
to stop the flow of affinity.
Release me!
These walls must come down.

I Thought it was Love

When lighter days morph
into meaningless nights,
it's like sunshine turning into rain.
I'm in my room, pen to paper,
candy-coated memories now distant,
love so temperate and fleeting.

Melting my inhibitions,
a recoiling turtle who fears
like a little child who runs to me.
She wraps her arms around my knees,
and grins a gap-toothed smile.

Recollections of an earlier time,
honeydew drops and butter kisses.
Now, a distant milestone in my rearview mirror,
jolting me out of my reverie,
a rude awakening to a midsummer's dream.
Vanquished by lies
in a puff of smoke and mirrors,
a sinister trick of some evil magician.

I am tilted, misunderstood,
heartstrings on my shoulders.
You pluck me, clever as a fox
but I won't dance to your tune anymore.
I am packing up my violin,
salvaging what's left of my shine.

Preserving my symphony
so I can play some other time,
I must go higher, deeper, wider.
I see portraits of the past
through a cloud of haze,
or is it a tunnel in my mind?

There is Purpose in the Pain

"Grief can be the garden of compassion.
If you keep your heart open through everything,
your pain becomes your greatest ally
in your life's search for love and wisdom."
—Rumi

"You have so much more to write," she said to me.
"Yes I know," I answered.

But sometimes the sword gets
heavy in my hand,
the veil of tears thick in my eyelashes.
We humans have a propensity
to shut down when grief
is too much for words.

Bitter roots, remorseful roots,
insecure roots.
Bittersweet aftertaste of misery
poured from desolate hearts.

We bottle up pain,
collecting the essence of strange flowers,
heaping them close
to our embittered hearts,
unaware that heartbreaks are gold nuggets
to be stored in life's vault.

At the ripe old age of wisdom,
will we learn that our pain
has given birth to our purpose.

The Siege

Pink ribbon stickers on bumpers
of cars, in emails and social media.
Pink pins and broaches on lapels.
Tiny pink flags flap in the autumn wind
at Mercy Medical Center under the hospital sign.

A leviathan lurks, his tail
sweeps one third of the shining
stars of heaven and lays them
at the watery feet of Long Island.
Eulogized, crushed hopes and dreams.
Mothers, sisters, aunts and cousins —
generations stalked by this faceless demon.

We tiptoe like school girls,
aware of what we eat.
Navigating around our diets,
traipsing through a field of forgotten
landmines.
Suspicious of the water,
shunning man-made foods and ingredients
we can barely pronounce.

I pull into the hospital parking lot.
Dread wraps me in a heavy cloak.
High tide, overpowering waves
that refuse to leave the shore,
drowning me in fear.
A roaring lion awakens
from someplace deep within me.
His roar gets louder
as I walk through the lobby
to the elevator.

In the breast surgeon's office,
I wait pensively, after months of uncertainty.
Cutting, packing, enduring the pain.
Local anesthesia, cold interior.
White washed walls and metal probes
Injecting and retracting.
More scanning and pressing of flesh.
I wait.

Good news — "Non-cancerous tissue,
yet I must operate."
Later, my surgeon will describe
the amount of flesh he removed from my breast.

I look in the mirror at the scar.
A crescent shaped half-moon
hugs my right areola.
At first angry looking,
then subtle with healing.
I have a strong urge to cover it.

Why do we cover scars?
Oblivious of the scars we may
have on our souls.

Scars

Crescent half moon
a memory of
an eight-month battle,
splayed on my right breast.
Sharp-edged sword —
scalpel, mistempered weapon
of my discomfort
and torture.

Our scars tell a story.
Childhood, childbirth,
wearing our fragile heart
on our sleeves,
exposed, naked.

Warriors have scars.
I want to be like the Dinka tribe
of South Sudan
or the Yoruba tribe in Nigeria,
unflinching as hot knife slices flesh
peeling back layers of vanity.

Warriors wear their scars
with pride. A testament,
whispering their
strength and courage.

Fear

"How many thousands of years have you been there."
—Ho Xuan Huong

You've died a thousand deaths.
Fear ain't fair!
It don't play by the rules.
It's like being in the belly of winter —
no coat, no shoes.

Fear is a stalker who stealthily
seizes her prey.
A thief who lurks in the intimate
shadows of your mind,
etching herself into gray and white matter.
Subtle, crackling viscerally deep,
she coils her limbs.
Ice particles or a crafty blend of hot and cold.
A paralyzer; immobilizing with her
deceptive web.

Her venom is slow,
engulfing, digesting.
She abuses even the most hardened soldiers.
They fall prey to her siege,
building fortresses brick by brick.

A lone assailant, sharp steel in hand,
metal hitting metal.
Frantic screams and blood.
She lingers long after the scars
have faded.

Promise of Blessings

*"Ever since happiness heard your name
it has been running through the streets
trying to find you."*
—Hafiz

Formed in the secret cavity,
you are swimming in possibilities.

Birthing is pain,
a gift of multiplicity —
the miracle of a seed or a young boy
with five loaves and two fish.

I am weighed in the balances,
a foretaste of how you envisioned me.
You tell me to throw my net
where the tide swells,
a huge catch,
heavy with the burden of promises.
These blessings want to overtake me.

Faith and fear, unlikely twins,
struggle within my womb.
When faith grabs the heels of fear,
destiny calls.

A Raven or a Dove?

On the cusp of transformation,
warm days meld into chilly nights.
Death plunders my apple blossoms
and majestic trees shed their glory.
Each day brings a new giant.
Friend or foe — sometimes you never know.

The drum beats louder, harder —
the steady percussion
of one heart to another.
I listen for the trumpet's
clarion call to wake me up.
We must all wake up.

I'm dreaming of flood waters again,
an eternal flow that chills my soul.
A steady stream of night visions
makes my bone tremble.
Huge wall of water.
We were always threatened by waters.
Even Noah had a way of escape.

In Clandestine Hours

*"Why do you circle the purple loneliness of night
and seldom blush before the sun."*
                    —Ho Xuan Huong

The moon creeps up over
my sleepy town
like a barn owl, staring
into the dark.
Quietness lingers, a thick fog
that lulls me to sleep,
bone weary.

Layers and layers of dreams,
but for some, the night is
a setting for their restlessness.
They haunt bars and strip clubs,
searching for the salve to heal
the man-sized hole in their souls.

We were made to create,
to bring forth life.
The mind is a battlefield,
at other times, barren —
a frustrated womb,
a walled off city on a hill.
The universe — our incubator.
Who will plant the seeds?

In the Fourth Watch of the Night

"The breeze at dawn has its secrets to tell you.
Don't go back to sleep."
—Rumi

These are the hours that pale tonight.
Cold dark days where time winds back.
Somber nights thick with the air of uncertainty,
my private Gethsemane.

Sometimes, at the edge of brokenness,
the lonely landscape of my heart
knows thinly veiled revelations,
but my mind can't yet comprehend
what my spirit already knows.

Truth speaks in a tight vein,
exposing flesh and marrow,
releasing wisdom, like the fragrance
of crushed petals.

It is a ladder of blessings
that spans height and depth,
where angels thread.

Night Visions

"The human body is composed in the airy balance
of cobwebs, cake batter and universe"
—Nynke Passi

Sharp intuition and discernment bestowed,
yet mundane tasks of every day
conflict my soul like steely fingers
around my neck
clutching, scraping, suffocating.
A clogged pipeline or a failed heart.
I must breathe. . .

You anointed my hands to pen these visions
of storms, portentous winds
and hearts failing out of fear.
At times, it's bitter medicine to my bones,
but how can I drink of the sweet
and not receive the bitter also?

Moon trails me by night,
clarity and truth by day.
My love waxes and wanes,
soars above the clouds
and expands within the cosmos of my heart,
swelling wide to high tide.
It thunders inside the electric
currents of Niagara,
suddenly ceasing.

The flow of the universe
pulls me out into the celestial.
Moonbeams and airships, flashes of light,
and I'm flying through tunnels,
falling through dark crevices.

A young woman gives a signal
and a huge entrance opens.
She enters, and I float
towards the secret room,
but the door slams shut.
Access Denied!!!

When the moon embraces the sun,
tides will turn.
Poseidon gets his revenge on the
inhabitants of the coast.
Leviathan waits, restlessly stirring,
loose from the abyss.
Change comes and with it judgment.
After the revolution,
blood moon rising.

My First Night in Tel Aviv

Brooding, dusky skies
stretch above me
like a calm blanket.
Cobalt blue, devoid of stars.
So close, its tranquility
engulfs me.

Head wrapped with the
knowledge that this world
is shrouded with vast mysteries. . .
We're different yet the same,
as identical as the color
of the blood in our veins.

A contrast between the modern
and the archaic.
Contemporary white buildings huddle
between animated streets, dust and concrete.
A familiar chord,
the vein of every city.

Midsummer's heat yields sultry
nights on the Mediterranean shore.
I feel balmy sand beneath my feet.
Graffiti screams vibrant colors
from a gritty abandoned building
as it overlooks the gentle rolling sea.
Two young boys wash the
salt from their bodies
at the standpipes.

I stand on jagged rocks
and observe the lit shoreline
of hotels and half-naked bodies
on the sand and think,
"I'm in the Holy Land."

A Man from Galilee

Tranquility.
Deep, calm and still
water rising
like warm spun gold
on a lonely pier.
Breakfast on Skydeck,
my face pressed to the glass.
Sunlight rests on my eyelids,
splashes the nearby dock
of the Caesar Hotel
in Galilee.

I am collecting early morning
expectations, divine connections
on this sacred journey.
Ephemeral yet abiding
heart to heart.
A bouquet of baby's breath,
violets, rose petals
and calla lilies,
a cherished gift of a lover.

A million times and more
I've longed to walk where you walked.
From the plains of the Jezreel Valley
and Acre to the Mediterranean shore.

These hills, rocks and dirt
have felt the warmth of your feet,
listened to the passion in your voice
and witnessed your miracles.
You are the bread of heaven.

Now, watching from my balcony,
I search for a trace of your presence
among the restless streets below.
Colorful lights pierce the night,
music everywhere, a mystical medley.

Van Morrison belts out his soul —
"Into the Mystic" and "Moondance."
I want to dance in the moonlight
on a magical night.
Silver specks of
moon dust in my hair
as I dip my toe
into the water's edge.
Rap, rock and reggae
are wrestling like immortal foes.

In a tavern beneath, a young
woman plays a guitar.
Her plaintive voice floats up,
wraps itself around my balcony.

Watchmen on the Western Wall

We walk the rugged stone path
through security and metal detectors,
stoic guards with swift gestures,
past a slender white cat.
She strolls up to dainty porcelain
dishes, laid out like a welcome mat.
A formation of steel tipped
boots on the ground, sweaty spines
and palms in sweltering heat.
Sturdy as palm trees reaching
for heaven with a promise
to God and country in front
of the Western Wall.

Leaning against the low iron gates
of the plaza entrance,
eyes searching, take their position.
Their intention, to avoid the gender partition.
They are intrigued by the faces,
nuances in colors and features.
Mesmerized by shapely lips
and hips under long skirts.

The blast of the *Shofar*, the chant
of the cantor, a clarion call
to dance. The young women
celebrate in groups. A circle
dance, hair and skirts blowing
in the summer breeze.

Sundown at the site of prayer
and pilgrimage. A balmy wind
wraps around my shoulders
like a comforting prayer shawl.
In the distance, close to the Western Wall,
a sea of yarmulkes undulates in waves
with a few beats in an off staccato rhythm.

Kabalat Shabbat, prayers lost
on adolescent caprice, as they
watch from a distance.
They say a Jewish boy is
spiritually mature at age thirteen,
an Awakening. This young man is more
focused on girl-watching.

Yad Vashem

Subdued, tentative steps echo
on tiled floors of *Yad VaShem.*
Haunted by shadows, stolen
hopes and dreams, these hallowed
halls cry out.

Photos, personal mementos
and heart wrenching testimonials
bridge the gap to the netherworld.
Forced calamity, the smell of torment
and violence still linger in the fibers
of humanity — the fabric of this
Jewish society.

We trail behind our sage tour guide,
Bernice. Her verbose and didactic
speeches now halted on sallow lips.
Hush tones of remembrance,
crimson and blue
like an invisible hand pressed
against her neck.

Asphyxiated, afflicted.
Her dark eyes peer at us
behind round, rimmed glasses.
Nightmarish phantoms, strokes of a Picasso
hung deliberately in the
annals of her memory,
the image of grandparents
who didn't survive the Holocaust.

She leaves us to explore
on our own.
In a somber, dimly lit
room, matchbox beds stacked
on top of each other
like poultry crates.
A snapshot of inhumanity,
cruelty and hate.

Hopelessness engraved on the
faces of the bone thin
and diseased.
Death expands her territory,
engulfs generations who slip into eternity.
Slaughtered on the altars
of Sobibor, Treblinka
and Auschwitz-Birkenau;
a burnt offering to the god
of the Fuhrer — and the children
suffered most.

Like shining stars,
detached from this callous world,
they suspend above the Children's
Memorial in quiet eeriness
as their names and ages are read.
Lambs in the embracing arms
of Janusz Korczak, now serving
his ghetto orphans in the afterlife.

Sun-kissed Kinneret

What if I had the power to stop time and motion?
To cause you to stand still in the sky,
sparkling orb in all your glory.
Would you still continue to shine?

Would you steadily draw awe from these lips
or rest upon the bows of stationary ships?
There would be no night, just day
in a world where only gold would stay.

The Universe is the Womb

*"Faith is the bird that feels the light
and sings when dawn is still dark."*
—Rabindranath Tagore

The universe is the womb
that births the seasons —
portal to all souls
in the earth, sea and sky.

Auburn, primrose, scarlet
and jade, vibrant
like on a canvas.
The setting sun, the backdrop.
Tulips break the earth
push past the melting snow.
Transforming this frostbitten temple —
buds of cherry and peach blossoms,
arms reaching up to the
oceans of the sky.

Life conceived out of dust.
I plant seeds in the fertile
soil of my mind —
a strange connection to the light.

Red Flag

Back bent, pricked fingertips
drip crimson, smeared on cotton.
Sweat and tears mingle.
Bare backs strapped-fifty-two lashes;
Spew the color of our soiled flag.
Broken necks, bodies hung limp,
swaying in the vile confederate wind.
Buck breaking, broken spirits.

Our trees are fallen,
plucked at the roots.
The fruit of our womb
stolen.
Our branches break,
Snapped limbs and body parts
severed joints and communities.
Who brought you from Egypt
in diseased ridden ships,
dear Jewel of the Nile?

Red Cry

Let's make America great again —
by breaking down the walls
that divide our ethnicities,
gender and disabilities.
Let's take ownership of our past atrocities,
broken promises and treaties.
Systematic trauma
in the minds of a people —
Lakota, Crow, Apache, Sioux,
Cheyenne, Cherokee, Navajo. . .

Massacre at Wounded Knee
and Bloody Island.
Fierce warriors fighting for survival.
Nature's protectors and guardians.

Standing Rock, not just another
standoff but a spiritual call
for retribution.
If not heeded, the blood of
our ancestors will soon cry out
from this land!

Sparring in the Age of Colorblindness

*"We just wanted to be alone
in that great shining emptiness."*
—Arthur C. Clarke

In the bliss of this vast earthiness
where love and hate spar
like two prize-fighters,
we wanted to assert our existence.
Bare knuckles clenching iron bars,
in the age of colorblindness
Thirteen years to contemplate fate.

About the Author

Marsha M. Nelson is a playwright and a poet. Her poem, "I Thought it was Love" won the Nassau County Poet Laureate Society 2016 contest. She has also written and directed several Resurrection Cantatas and Christmas plays. Poems in this book were previously published in the *NCPLS Review, the PPA Literary Review, the Long Island Quarterly, Poet's Almanac 2017*, and *Bards Annual 2016*.

Marsha is a world traveler and has explored Barbados, Trinidad, England, Wales, Spain, Israel, Canada, Turks and Caicos. Her bucket list includes Ethiopia, Egypt, India, Korea, China (Great Wall), Australia (Outback), Italy and France (Eiffel Tower.)

Since childhood, she has always loved animals. Her early memories include visiting her Dad in Arima, Trinidad and enjoying the animals in his yard. "On one visit, he announced to my brother, sister and I that he had purchased three geese and named them after us. We spent that visit being chased by those mischievous critters. My Dad also had a talking parrot who loved to eat mangoes. He had birds, parakeets, rabbits and of course dogs. He loved German Shepherds, and when they had puppies, I would be in puppy heaven." Marsha's early childhood experiences lead her into a career with animals. She owns and operates a dog grooming business called "Luv'n Pooches and Pals Mobile Dog Grooming."

www.ingramcontent.com/pod-product-compliance
Lightning Source LLC
Chambersburg PA
CBHW020943100426
42741CB00006BA/841